BEACON SERMON OUTLINE SERIES

SERMON OUTLINES
— ON —
Lessons
from the
Old Testament

GENE WILLIAMS

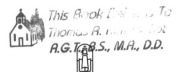

This Book Belongs To
Thomas R. ....
A.G.T.G.B.S., M.A., D.D.

Beacon Hill Press of Kansas City
Kansas City, Missouri

Copyright 2003 by
Beacon Hill Press of Kansas City

ISBN 083-412-0674

Printed in the
United States of America

Cover Design: Paul Franitza

Library of Congress Cataloging-in-Publication Data

Williams, Gene, 1932-
  Sermon outlines on lessons from the Old Testament / Gene Williams.
     p. cm. — (Beacon sermon outline series)
  ISBN 0-8341-2067-4 (pbk.)
  1. Bible. O.T.—Sermons—Outlines, syllabi, etc. 2. Christian life—Biblical teaching. I. Title.
II. Series.

  BS1199.C43W55 2003
  251'.02—dc21

                                                              2003011067

10 9 8 7 6 5 4 3 2 1

CONTENTS

INTRODUCTION

Sermon Outlines from the Old Testament

The Old Testament is rich in great preaching material. While we do not want to place less emphasis on the wonderful gospel of the New Testament, we must not overlook the treasures to be found in the Old Testament.

In these 39 books that God has carefully presented to us, we begin to see the picture of His will for humankind. The picture will unfold in three areas of emphasis.

1. The personalities of the Old Testament teach us some powerful lessons.
2. Jewish people have always looked to these writings for encouragement and hope. So it is understandable that we will find some great pastoral truths in these pages.
3. We will also be challenged by some of the great lessons we will discover.

A pastor who will spend time in this section of God's Word will find a veritable mother lode of material. The outlines in this volume are not presented in a series format but could very easily be organized in that manner.

In order to fully appreciate the message of the New Testament, we must have an understanding of the Old Testament. Enrich the lives of your people by taking these truths, mixing them with prayer and presenting them lovingly to your people.

Introduction to Pastoral Messages

There are some wonderful pastoral truths in the Old Testament. This is especially true of the Psalms. So we will take a brief look at those. Since many people struggle to discover God's will, it is important that they are given some simple truths to use in that discovery.

It is encouraging to be reminded that God is in control of everything in our lives. It is also encouraging to know that He wants us to enjoy life. In a day when there is so much pressure, these two messages can be very uplifting to weary people.

THE SECURITY OF TRUSTING GOD

Psalm 91

Introduction

    A. This is one of the most beautiful pieces of literature ever written.
- 1. This psalm, along with Ps. 23, Isa. 40, 55, and John 14, offers comfort.
- 2. Its beauty is not just in the use of words and punctuation marks but also in its message of hope.

    B. David had made a great discovery and shared it in this passage.
- 1. David had found a source of strength that helped him face life's difficulties.
- 2. In this psalm he shares the truth that enabled him to live confidently and joyfully.
- 3. Read the scripture: Ps. 91.

    C. In our world today we need to discover the truth David is conveying.
- 1. There will be pressures in life, but help is available.
- 2. He tells us simply where to go for help.

I. David Points Out That God Is the Source of Safety (vv. 1-2)

    A. David had discovered this refuge personally.
- 1. Note how many times he uses the personal pronoun in verse 2.
- 2. Verse 2 is a statement of fact, and everything else in this psalm is built upon this.

    B. God is a refuge from the penalty of sin.
- 1. We cannot ignore the reality of sin and its related problems.
- 2. The offer extended in 1 John 1:9 is very clear.
- 3. Jesus came into the world to provide us with a refuge from the penalty of sin.

C. God is a refuge from peril and danger (Ps. 91:3).
1. Many things lie in wait to trap, deceive, and defeat us.
2. If we stay close to Him, nothing can defeat us.
3. Verses 1 and 4 give us precious peace.

II. David Points Out That God Is the Place of Strength (v. 2)

A. A fortress is not just a refuge but also a stronghold. It holds back that which would capture and defeat us.
B. God is a fortress in times of temptation.
1. Paul pointed this out in 1 Cor. 10:13.
2. This is what David is addressing in Ps. 91:11-12.
3. God has the final say in everything that comes into our lives.
C. If we are going to be victorious in life's battle and enjoy the songs of David, we must accept God's strength and care.

III. David Points Out That God Is the Place of Sufficiency (vv. 14-16)

A. God can and will meet every need of our lives.
1. No one has invented a new need.
2. God gives permanent security to those who respond to Him.
3. What do you need that God cannot supply?
B. Through the ages humankind has found this place of sufficiency and safety.
1. In Dan. 3:17, the Hebrew children claimed the safety of God.
2. In Phil. 4:19, Paul wrote that our God will supply everything we need.

Conclusion

A. Where are you placing your trust? Everyone trusts something.
B. Where is your place of refuge? Everyone needs one.
C. I can recommend to you what David is promising. There is great security in trusting God for everything in our lives.

THE PRACTICE OF HIS PRESENCE

Psalm 84

Introduction

    A. Why do we go to church, and why do we worship God?

    B. It is interesting to consider the attitudes people have about going to church and worshiping God.

        1. For some it is drudgery—a chore to be performed.

        2. For some it is an obligation like paying bills.

        3. For others, worshiping God is a pure joy.

        4. For others, it is a normal part of their lives. They practice God's presence just like breathing.

    C. David spoke to that in Ps. 84.

        1. He wrote this psalm when Absalom forced him to leave the city and his place of worship (2 Sam. 15).

        2. David seemed to be most concerned about leaving God's house.

        3. Read the scripture: Ps. 84.

I. Look at David's Desire for God's House (vv. 1-2)

    A. David longed to be in the house of the Lord.

        1. Do we feel this way today? Is there a longing to be in God's house?

        2. Those who truly love Him long for that which is designed for His glory.

    B. David longed for God's presence (v. 2).

        1. He desperately wanted to be in God's presence (Ps. 42:1-2).

        2. It was not so much the courts of the Lord as the living God himself.

    C. The sparrows were doing what David longed to do (84:3).

        1. They were at ease in His presence.

        2. David would rather live in a bird's nest near God's altar than in a palace far away.

II. Praising God Is a Way of Life (vv. 4-7)

A. It is no imposition to serve God when we love Him.

  1. David blessed those who practiced God's presence and praised His name.

  2. We should spend as much time as possible practicing for what we will do throughout eternity (see Rev. 7:9-12).

B. There is strength in God's presence (Ps. 84:5). Those who practice His presence find Him to be a spiritual fortress (Ps. 46).

C. Surviving difficult situations depends upon our closeness to Him (84:6-7).

  1. The valley of Baca represents weeping and difficult times in our lives.

  2. Those with an established close relationship with God are prepared for bad times.

III. Look at the Choice David Made (vv. 10-11)

A. Holy hearts take great delight in holy duties.

  1. David really loved God.

  2. It is never a chore to do the things that we love. Illustrate with something you enjoy doing.

B. We not only find pleasure but also find God's protection (v. 11). We walk daily in the "protective custody" of God.

C. Wonderful blessings are ours (v. 11).

Conclusion

A. Blessed are those who trust in God (v. 12). Those who practice His presence and learn to trust Him, praise Him, and walk with Him, discover they have life's best.

B. Why do we come to church? We come to worship Him and build a relationship that enables us to practice His presence daily.

The Wonder of the Lord

Psalm 139

Introduction

    A. This psalm is sometimes referred to as "the crown" of all psalms. It contains some of the great encouragement that we see in Pss. 23 and 91.

    B. David is speaking eloquently of God and His nature.

        1. Two of the attributes of God that we need to realize in our lives form the heart of this message: He is omniscient—He knows everything; He is omnipresent—He is everywhere.

        2. He also calls to our minds that God is personally concerned with all of the details of our lives (139:13-16).

        3. He points out that we can have a special relationship with God (vv. 17-18).

        4. He concludes with a prayer worthy of each one of us (vv. 23-24).

        5. Read the scripture: Ps. 139.

    C. When we begin to think as David thought, we will begin to live as he lived—in joy and confidence. Note Pss. 118 and 121.

I. David Pointed Out That God Knows Us (vv. 1-5)

    A. David was excited that God truly knew him.

        1. David said that God looked at him and examined his motives (v. 1).

        2. God knew every detail of David's life (vv. 2-3).

        3. God knew his thoughts before they became words (v. 4).

    B. What was true of David is also true of you and me today.

        1. God knows our true selves. No one can tell Him anything about us.

        2. He bases His judgment on what He knows—not on what others think or say.

        3. God knows our thoughts even before they become words.

C. David saw himself surrounded by God like a well-fortified city (v. 5). We may not understand why or how. But the fact remains that He surrounds us.

II. God Is with Us (vv. 6-12)
A. David was in the protective custody of God.
  1. *The Living Bible* reads, "This is too glorious, too wonderful to believe! . . . I can *never* get away from my God! If I go up to heaven, you are there; if I go down to the place of the dead, you are there. If I ride the morning winds to the farthest oceans, even there your hand will guide me, your strength will support me. . . . even darkness cannot hide from God; to you the night shines as bright as day. Darkness and light are both alike to you."
  2. Neither the wings of the morning nor the uttermost parts of the sea can carry us out of the reach of God's right hand to heal and to hold.
B. One of the most encouraging facts of life is that God is with us.
  1. Remember how the angel interpreted Isa. 7:14 when he spoke to Joseph in Matt. 1:23.
  2. Wherever we are, God is.

III. God Is Personally Concerned About His People (vv. 13-16)
A. David said that God had designed and made him (v. 13). We are not mass-produced. We are custom-made.
B. This is another reason for us to accept our best self and feel a sense of real worth. If we determine to do His will, that will solve a lot of life's problems.
C. These are precious thoughts to David and us (vv. 17-18).

Conclusion
David's closing prayer is worthy of each one of us (vv. 23-24). May God help us to be what He designed us to be.

Living a Life of Praise

Psalm 150

Introduction

    A. The Book of Psalms is a very special portion of the Word of God.
1. It is the most read book in the Bible.
2. Martin Luther called the Psalms a Bible in miniature.
3. Every emotion of humankind from exhilarating praise to the deepest despair is evidenced in the Psalms.
4. One-third of the 263 Old Testament passages quoted in the New Testament are from the Psalms.
5. With these thoughts in mind, we are studying the closing psalm. Read the scripture: Ps. 150.

    B. Why is so much emphasis placed on praise? We will examine three simple reasons. Each one is very appropriate.

I. People Who Count Their Blessings Have No Time or Tendency to Complain

    A. When we give our minds to thanking God for what He has given to us, we will not take time to complain about our needs. Each one of us has more blessings than we deserve.

    B. When we are busy thanking God for His goodness to us, it is difficult to focus on the faults and failures of others.
1. We are grateful that He has "overloved" our failures.
2. Recognizing His grace to us enables us to pass grace on to others.

    C. People who complain, criticize, and are dominated by pessimism are not counting their blessings. When we count our blessings, there is no time to complain.

    D. To live a life of praise glorifies God in our daily lives.

II. It Is Good for Us to Praise God

    A. It is emotionally healthy to praise Him.
1. We withdraw from wrong and respond to what is right.

      2. Those who open up in praise have a ray of sunshine in their minds.

  B. It is good for us mentally to praise God.

      1. We do not get tired of the things that are good and right.

      2. Our minds are clearer when they are fixed on positive things.

  C. It is good for us spiritually to praise God.

      1. A positive attitude enables us to trust Him more and draw closer to Him.

      2. People who complain do not trust Him. They miss His gentle guidance.

      3. Illustration: At Kadesh Barnea in Num. 14, the children of Israel had moved into a complaining mode, and they lost sight of God's guidance.

III. We Are the Only Creation That Can Make a Rational Decision to Praise God

  A. Other parts of creation display His handiwork.

      1. David declares this in Ps. 19.

      2. The universe shows His mighty power.

      3. Mountains and seas display His majesty.

      4. Birds and animals show His tenderness as they trust His care.

  B. Only humankind knows God's love and can return something to Him. People who are alive in the Lord cannot help but praise Him.

Conclusion

David wrote that our praise is God ordained. (Read Ps. 8.) God wants our praise. So throughout the Psalms, David, a man after God's own heart, calls continuously for praise. Read Ps. 150 again.

God Is in Control

Daniel 6:10-23

Introduction
A. When we look at the world in which we live, we might want to ask if anyone is in control. Wars and rebellion are erupting in many places. Many of our city streets have become battlegrounds. Perhaps the worst situation is the heartache that reaches into so many homes. It is easy to ask if anyone is in charge.

B. We can be sure that our Heavenly Father is still very much in command.
1. While humankind may create havoc because of sinful hearts, we can be sure that God will exercise His sovereignty when He chooses to do so.
2. Some people worry about the end of the world. But God will have the final say about that.
3. Personally, if we will let Him, God will still maintain control of our lives.

C. Today's text clearly establishes that God has the final word. Read the scripture: Dan. 6:10-23.

I. The Bible Clearly Illustrates the Sovereignty of God
A. The case of Noah is the first illustration. In Gen. 6—9 we read about Noah. Humankind got out of control. God took charge and regained control.

B. The case of Joseph illustrates God's sovereignty. We read about Joseph in Gen. 37—50. Joseph's brothers would have done away with him. God decided to use him for the salvation of his people. Joseph recognized God's plans in all of the events (Gen. 45:5).

C. The story of Daniel illustrates God's sovereignty (Dan. 6). Daniel was a man of prayer, and his enemies wanted to destroy him (vv. 4-5). The king recognized that Daniel's God was special (v. 16). God delivered His servant (vv. 21-23).

D. The New Testament continues with the same emphatic theme: God is in charge. While His enemies crucified Jesus, God had the final word and resurrected Him. Paul and Silas were imprisoned, but God delivered them (Acts 16).

II. Who Is in Control Today?

A. Do we have the right to the same confidence in our day? The Bible clearly teaches that we do. All that God ever was, He still is today (see Heb. 13:8).

B. Look at some scripture passages that encourage our hearts:
1. Ps. 24:1 reminds us that the earth belongs to the Lord.
2. 2 Cor. 4:7-18 encourages us to hold steady in difficulty.
3. 1 Cor. 10:13 explains our hope during temptation.
4. Jude 24 and 25 contain a wonderful promise.

C. Each of these verses clearly establishes that God is in control. We need to learn to trust God in every aspect of our lives. In His Word God is telling us to love and trust Him and He will take care of us.

Conclusion

A. Many people in today's world are ill at ease and at the point of despair. We need to listen to God's Word and understand that there is hope. God's people know that He is in control, and that means that all will be well. Peter encourages us to praise God for the living hope that we have (1 Pet. 1:3-7).

B. According to God's Word, nothing on earth can separate us from God's love (Rom. 8:38-39).

C. Realizing that God is in control should produce incredible peace in our lives.

D. If possible, close with a song such as "God Will Take Care of You" or a song or chorus with a similar message.

The Lord Will Provide

Genesis 22:1-14

Introduction
   A. Sooner or later each of us must decide if he or she truly
      believes God. The lesson in trusting God is clearly
      demonstrated in today's scripture. Read the scripture:
      Gen. 22:1-14.
   B. Look at the story of Isaac. He had been born to Abraham
      and Sarah in their old age (chap. 21). He had brought
      great joy to them (vv. 6-7).

I. God Tested Abraham's Commitment (v. 2)
   A. Abraham's alternatives were clear. He could have said
      that God was asking too much, or he could obey God.
      1. Abraham's life pattern had been to have absolute
         trust in God (chaps. 12—13).
      2. The patterns of our lives are what we follow in times
         of stress and pressure.
   B. Abraham followed God's directions and made the sacri-
      fice (22:9-10). While Abraham made the sacrifice, God
      provided the ram (vv. 12-13).
   C. God did not ask too much of Abraham. Nor does He ask
      too much of us. What He asks us to do, He enables us to
      do.

II. The Scriptural Pattern Is That God Provides What We Need to Please Him
   A. This is clearly illustrated in the story of Elijah in 1 Kings
      17.
      1. God had led Elijah to the Kerith Brook.
      2. While he was in that desolate area, God provided for
         his needs (v. 6).
      3. When the brook dried up, God had another plan for
         Elijah (v. 7).
   B. God provided for the widow to take care of His servant
      Elijah.

       1. Famine and death seemed very evident (v. 12).
       2. Because of the widow's obedience, God provided for her family and for Elijah.
  C. The New Testament picture is the same. The Lord will provide.
       1. They brought water to Him, and He provided wine (John 2).
       2. A lad brought a small lunch. Jesus fed a multitude (chap. 6).
       3. They brought an empty net. He loaded their boat (chap. 21).
  D. The Bible is full of illustrations that God responds to our faith in His ability to provide for us. In Acts 27:23-25 Paul stated his faith that God would get them safely to land. It happened just as God had promised.

III. The Good News Is That God Still Provides for Believers Today

  A. He provides whatever is needed to enable us to please Him when the pattern of our lives is one of absolute trust in Him.
  B. Look at what He provides for us.
       1. Forgiveness for every sin we have ever committed
       2. The Holy Spirit to fill us with His presence
       3. A purpose for life's journey
       4. Provisions for the journey
       5. Power for the problems we will face
  C. Our call is to trust God and let Him provide what we need to fulfill His will.

Conclusion

  A. The key to experiencing God's best comes through having the faith to trust Him and never question His ability to take care of us.
  B. We simply bring what we have in faith to God and let Him add it to His storehouse. We set up a joint account with Him from which we can draw all that we need for living.

LESSONS FROM A POOR WIDOW

1 Kings 17:7-23

Introduction

    A. The lessons in this message spring from the story of the prophet Elijah and his meeting with a poor widow.

        1. Because of King Ahab's evil and idolatrous acts (1 Kings 16:30, 32-33), God sent Elijah to tell him a drought would afflict the land (17:1). God then led Elijah to the Brook Kerith, where ravens fed him (vv. 5-6).

        2. As time passed, the brook dried up and God needed someone to care for Elijah. He extended this wonderful privilege to a poor widow.

    B. Read the scripture: 1 Kings 17:7-23.

        1. The encounter in verse 10 took place at the well, the town's meeting place.

        2. The drought made the fields barren; the pressure of famine was affecting everyone, including Elijah. God's prophet asked an apparently selfish request of the woman (v. 11). Her response was normal (v. 12). Still the prophet persisted.

I. Lesson One: God's Ways Are Sometimes Beyond Our Understanding

    A. In that situation, they were far beyond the widow's understanding.

        1. She had very little. Yet Elijah was asking her to share. She knew she did not have enough to feed both her family and Elijah, and she could not understand why Elijah made such a request of her.

        2. If she had known what was going to happen, faith would not have been necessary.

    B. That same lesson is taught elsewhere.

        1. In 2 Kings 5, the leper Naaman had to bathe in the muddy Jordan because that is what God said to do.

        2. In John 9, Jesus put mud on the eyes of the blind man and told him to "wash in the Pool of Siloam" (v. 7).

C. We must learn that sometimes God's ways are a mystery to us and all we can do is just trust and obey. The widow did this and was truly glad she did.

II. Lesson Two: When We Trust and Obey, God Takes Responsibility for Success

A. Until the widow stepped out in faith and trusted something she did not understand, her future was predictable—failure, failure (1 Kings 17:12).
1. It was not her place to find flour and oil to meet the need. The plan was God's. He always takes responsibility for obedient people.
2. At the Red Sea, Moses held the rod but God parted the waters. Jesus' miracles used the same formula: fill the waterpots, let the nets down, and so on.
3. Verse 13 is the key to this—"But first . . ." Jesus was saying the same thing in Matt. 6:33.
B. In our lives today, God is responsible for adequacy. Whatever He leads us to do, He will enable us to do.

III. Lesson Three: When God's Honor Is at Stake, He Does More than Imagined

A. While it is true that the provisions never ran out (1 Kings 17:16), God gave the widow an added blessing. When her son died, God restored him through Elijah (vv. 17-23). She trusted, obeyed, and was blessed.
B. Today, people who trust God and obey Him experience more than they ever imagined. Our call from God to acts of faith may be beyond our understanding. If we obey, we will be blessed.

Conclusion

The lessons from this poor widow are not easy to practice. However, they are standard procedure in God's Word, and they still work today.

God Really Cares About You

Isaiah 49:8-16

Introduction

    A. Some people look at the future with questions. Believers look with confidence.

        1. Our attitude toward God determines how we live today. The level of our joy in life will be in direct ratio to our faith in God's Word. Read the scripture: Isa. 49:8-16.

        2. Although we face an unknown future, we can be sure that while we may not always know where God is, He knows just where we are.

    B. As we move into situations we have never experienced, we could have some frightening times.

        1. At times we may ask, "God, where are You?" and we may wonder, "Why is this happening to me?"

        2. Some people will wonder if what is going on in their lives matters to God. While there are 6 billion people on earth, each one of us is important to God.

I. Look at the Situation That Existed for Israel

    A. They were in Babylonian captivity. Jerusalem had been destroyed, and they had been taken to a strange land. Their heartaches abounded as their captors treated them unmercifully.

    B. The situation seemed hopeless. They wondered where God was.

        1. God had not left them; they had left Him.

        2. God gave them some great promises (vv. 8-11). They should have been happy (v. 13). Instead, they were afraid and felt forsaken (v. 14).

        3. God then gave them a wonderful promise (vv. 15-16). God was telling them how He felt in a way they could understand (v. 15).

II. God Exhibited His Care for Them

    A. Surely the 400 years of silence between the Old and New Testaments made it seem as though God had forgotten them. "When the time had fully come, God sent his Son" (Gal. 4:4). Christmas is the booming voice of God telling us He still loves us.

B. Jesus was a caring Savior.
1. See Him weeping over Jerusalem (Luke 19:41).
2. See Him moved with compassion as He looked at a needy crowd (Matt. 14:14).
3. See Him concerned about a man who had been crippled for 38 years (John 5).
4. Even after His resurrection He still exhibited compassion for the frustrated disciples (John 21).

C. God sent Jesus to pay the price for our sins. This was the ultimate demonstration of the way He cares for us. But He also sent Jesus to manifest His love for all who are in distress or difficulty.

III. God Still Cares Today

A. In Heb. 13:8 we read, "Jesus Christ is the same yesterday and today and forever." All that Jesus ever was, He still is; all that He is, He will be. We can walk into the future with absolute confidence in Him. He is still the Shepherd who goes looking for His sheep and stands at the door of the sheepfold to anoint our hurts.

B. When things go wrong, the sky is dark, and there is no hope in sight, remember that you are inscribed on the palm of your Heavenly Father's hand.

C. He who created you and this marvelous world looks upon you as though you were the only person alive.

Conclusion

Remember, as you enter the unknown future, you may not be sure of many things, but you can be absolutely sure that you matter to God.

Something Beautiful

Isaiah 61:1-3

Introduction
    A. While John the Baptist was in prison, he sent a messenger to Jesus for answers. He was in Herod's prison and wanted something to give his life meaning. (See his question and Jesus' answer in Luke 7:19-23.) Jesus' answer gave him the courage to face death.

    B. Today, many are looking for something to give them hope. God's Word can do this for those who receive what it says. Read the scripture: Isa. 61:1-3.

    C. This chapter from Isaiah was given to encourage the Israelites while they were in Babylonian captivity. It is clearly a prophecy of the deliverance that would come through the Messiah. Jesus alluded to this in Luke 4:16-20. This is a message of hope that makes beautiful lives for God's people.

I. Good News to the Poor (v. 1)
    A. God's message is one with a great common denominator. In God's eyes, everyone is of equal value (see Deut. 10:17). Peter reflected this in Acts 10:30-35.

    B. It is good news to know that everyone is welcome in Jesus' presence and that all He has is available to us. No one is left out.

II. Good News for the Brokenhearted (v. 1)
When we break a limb, we wrap it for comfort and freedom from pain. Jesus came to "bind up the brokenhearted." Bleeding hearts are bound in His love so they can heal. Those whose hearts are broken because of sin find healing in Jesus.

III. Good News for Those in Captivity (v. 1)
    A. The captive Jews finally experienced their relief from bondage. King Cyrus opened the gates that had held them captive for 70 years.

1. This captivity was worse than the 400 years in Egypt. The Syrians deported their captives in order to destroy their nationalism. They were also cruel and physically mutilated their captives.
        2. God was telling them that He had deliverance for all who would believe.
    B. Sin is a cruel taskmaster for those held in its captivity. It will be destructive both physically and eternally. Jesus has conquered sin and destroyed the power of Satan to rule over our lives (see Rom. 6:1-7 and John 8).

IV. Good News for Those Who Mourn (v. 2)

   A. Those who weep can experience God's comforting presence (see John 14). We do not mourn as though we have no hope (see Rom. 15:13). In Col. 1:27 Paul wrote, Christ is our "hope of glory."
   B. If it had not been for the coming of Jesus, we would be without hope. But Jesus, the Messiah, has come with hope for all of those whose hearts are broken.

V. Good News: God's People Will Be Vindicated (v. 3)

   A. He gives beauty instead of ashes and "the oil of gladness instead of mourning." The ashes of repentance will bring the crown of His blessings.
   B. God wants His people to wear "garment[s] of praise instead of a spirit of despair." This represents the beautiful garments worn at Thanksgiving feasts rather than the heavy garments worn during funerals. While God's people have problems, they never despair.
   C. Believers are like "oaks of righteousness" that display God's splendor. The oak is a symbol of the strength and permanence God's people are to have.

Conclusion

God has planned and provided beautiful lives for those who listen and respond. Is God doing something beautiful in your life? He wants to do that for you.

Introduction to Messages from Personalities

The people of the Old Testament were just as human as we are today. While many things have changed, human needs and the nature of people have not. Because of this we can learn some great truths from ancient personalities. These messages are designed to teach such truths from the lives of some of these individuals.

The outlines in this section can be customized to reach certain age-groups whether they are children, youth groups, or adults. It is important, however, to remember that the lessons taught by the texts involved are applicable to everyone in your congregation.

A REASON FOR BEING: ESTHER

Esther 4:1-16

Introduction
- A. For all of us there comes a time when we need to focus on our reason for being. Focused lives have more penetrating power than unfocused ones. Illustration: Some flashlights can be focused so they can further penetrate the darkness. When they are not focused, they can only show what is nearby. In today's world the darkness needs to be driven back.
- B. We have a golden opportunity to make a difference. There is something each one of us can do. The situation is not as hopeless as the enemy would have us believe. To bring about a change we need to follow Esther's example. Read the scripture: Esther 4:1-16.

I. The Need Is Very Clear
- A. The need in today's scripture passage is very clear. Haman obviously represents the forces of Satan. He had cunningly crafted a way to destroy God's people.
- B. The need in our world today is very obvious. The penalty of death and destruction hangs over every person. Since Satan is so sly, many people do not understand the danger. As a result there is a great disaster hanging over everyone's head. Someone needs to rise to the challenge to make a difference.

II. In Today's Scripture Esther Got the Message
- A. As Mordecai spoke to her, God laid the burden upon her heart. Note Esther's initial response in verse 11 when she said it was too much to ask. Finally, the picture became clear, and she heard the call (vv. 13-14). God always finds someone who will rise to the challenge. We need to let Him use us today.
- B. Esther brought her life into focus (v. 16). This is a commitment God always honors. Illustration: David made

that commitment in facing Goliath (1 Sam. 17). The priests made that commitment when they stepped into the Jordan (Josh. 3). When Esther abandoned herself to God's assignment, He took over.

C. He will do the same with us today. When we surrender ourselves to God, He takes responsibility for the outcome. We need to come to the place Esther did and find something worth dying for.

D. Esther prepared herself for her assignment the best way she knew (Esther 4:16).

III. Get Ready for Great Joy

A. Life's ultimate experience is knowing that God has used us. When lives are focused, the darkness is penetrated and someone sees the light of deliverance. There is marvelous joy in being that used by God.

B. Imagine the joy Esther experienced when she was given the power to free her people (8:8). The fears she expressed in 4:11 never came to pass. Imagine her joy when the celebration (8:15-17) took place.

C. We have the same opportunity to know great joy by pursuing our reason for being—being used of God.

Conclusion

A. One of today's great tragedies is that we can live a mediocre life and get by with it. Why should we settle for mediocrity when we can focus on our reason for being and experience great joy?

B. Our call is to be God's instrument of deliverance to a world under death's penalty. When we let Him use us, great joy is the result.

C. God has great plans for people who will focus their lives on His plan and let nothing turn them aside.

Obedience—the Only Way: Naaman

2 Kings 5:1-14

Introduction

A. God has opened the Kingdom's door to anyone who wants to enjoy His blessings. Most people want to enjoy the pleasure of God's friendship. To enjoy these benefits there are some conditions to be met. It is important for us to learn that the only way to experience God's blessings is through obedience to His instructions.

B. The story of Naaman in today's passage illustrates clearly how vital obedience is. Read the scripture: 2 Kings 5:1-14. God did not meet Naaman's needs without obedience nor will He meet ours without the same.

I. Look at Naaman's Condition

A. Naaman was a man of high standing in the government. As captain of the king's host, he would have been next to the king in power. Naaman had one critical problem. He was a leper. It has been said that while Naaman was as great as the world could make him, the poorest person in the kingdom would not have traded skin with him. His story is proof that no one is out of reach of life's worst calamities.

B. Naaman is typical of many people in today's world.
  1. There are many good, powerful people who suffer from dreadful diseases.
  2. There is a close parallel between the destructiveness of leprosy with that of sin. Both begin as small, seemingly insignificant infections that spread disastrously.

II. Look at the Proposition Given to Naaman

A. He preferred to wash in what he considered to be cleaner waters (v. 12).
  1. He wanted to do things his own way.
  2. God's prophet, Elisha, did not promise healing in the rivers Naaman chose. Healing would only come when he obeyed God-given instructions.

B. Today, many people act like Naaman.
   1. They want God's blessings, but they want them on their terms. Some look for a more respectable way to become people of God.
   2. The only way to know God's forgiveness is through Jesus (1 John 1:9). Illustration: The story of Nicodemus makes it clear that being good and religious is not enough (John 3).

III. Look at the Results of Naaman's Submission
A. His servants intervened in his situation (2 Kings 5:13).
   1. It is essential that we have those who help keep us on course.
   2. It is easy to enjoy God's blessings if we obey. Obedience and faith are intertwined. Disobedience is a statement of disbelief that is an insult to God's integrity.
B. When Naaman obeyed, wonderful things happened (v. 14). He went to the place to which the prophet had directed him and performed the act that had been described. He received what he needed only through complete obedience.
C. This is still the way grace from God is received today. It takes complete surrender to God's will to enjoy His blessings. God does not make bargains with anyone. When we are obedient to His guidance, God gives us the very "best from the land" (Isa. 1:19).

Conclusion
A. If Naaman were to ask you what you thought about the decision he had to make, what would you tell him?
B. If you want to enjoy the pleasure of God's blessings and an eternity with Him, you must also be obedient to what He is telling you right now.

Forgive and Be Forgiven: Joseph

Genesis 50:15-21

Introduction

A. If you want to be truly miserable, carry a grudge against someone. Whether you are right or wrong, you will end up being the loser. Your spirit will become bitter, cynical, and sarcastic. Your soul, personality, and even sometimes your body may be crippled by harboring the attitude of unforgiveness. Today's scripture provides a perfect guideline for us in learning to forgive. Read Gen. 50:15-21.

B. In order to enjoy life's best, we must live with an attitude of forgiveness. We can be absolutely sure that someone, sometime will offend us. Until we forgive that person, we will be under great pressure. Jesus alerts us to the critical nature of forgiveness in Matt. 6:14-15.

C. The story in today's scripture is a great example of how we are to forgive.

I. Joseph's Story Begins in Gen. 37

A. In the beginning Joseph's brothers wanted to harm him.
   1. They were jealous of him.
   2. They plotted carefully how they could get rid of him.

B. God had other plans for Joseph and protected him.
   1. He protected him in a time of temptation (Gen. 39).
   2. He opened the door for him to rise to prominence in Egypt (Gen. 40—41).
   3. God made Joseph into a powerful person.
   4. As a result of the famine, Joseph's brothers became subject to his power.

C. Joseph genuinely forgave those who had wronged him.

D. Joseph had a proper concept of himself as a human being (v. 19).

E. Joseph reflected the same spirit that Jesus modeled on the Cross (Luke 23:34).

II. The Lesson from God's Word Is Very Clear

A. The Bible commands us to live forgiving lives.
   1. There are 103 references to forgiveness in the Bible.
   2. Some references include Col. 3:12-13; Eph. 4:30-32; and Matt. 5:21-25.

B. We are not forced to forgive but unless we do God will not forgive us.
   1. There are many things in life that are important, but we are not forced to do, such as love, work, respect others, and so forth.
   2. When a person insists on getting revenge, he or she forfeits God's precious presence.
   3. We cannot have God's best and hold on to a grudge. God wants both hands.

C. We are to follow the examples of Jesus and Joseph.
   1. People who mistreat us do not really understand what they are doing.
   2. Give them the benefit of any doubt.
   3. When we put our pride on the altar, we will solve many problems.
   4. Let God settle the score just as He did with Joseph.

D. We pay a high price when we fail to forgive.
   1. Satan wants to make us think we are making someone else pay. That is not so.
   2. It costs us our peace of mind. Without rest we will never find true peace.
   3. It costs us the joys of life. We cannot relax and enjoy life without forgiveness.
   4. It costs us the presence of God. He will not dwell in a bitter heart.
   5. It can cost us our souls. (See Jesus' promise in Matt. 6:14-15.)

Conclusion

If you want to live miserable lives, carry unforgiveness in your heart. To enjoy life at its best, take the initiative and forgive. Follow the example of Christ. He is our supreme Model for forgiveness. Remember, the greatest gift you can ever give to yourself is to forgive others.

An Example of Obedience: Elisha

2 Kings 2:1-15

Introduction

A. The prophet Elisha illustrates a condition that pastors covet for their people. This is a lifestyle that raises us to our greatest potential. It is a vivid illustration of what happens when people are obedient to God. His will is not always convenient, understandable, or comfortable for us. Those who make a commitment to God and stay with that commitment have incredible experiences with Him. Read 2 Kings 2:1-15.

B. This story demonstrates the fact that individual personalities differ and their work for God can be different.
   1. Elijah was a stern, forceful, rugged loner.
   2. Elisha was a gentle, kind man who loved being with people. He fulfilled his mission by helping others.
   3. God takes each of us where we are. As we respond He shapes us into His plan.

I. Elisha Responded to God's Call (1 Kings 19:19-21)

A. God had future plans for him.
   1. Note that God made sure Elisha knew His plan for him (1 Kings 19:19). Prov. 3:5-6 is very true.
   2. Isa. 3:21 is another wonderful verse to remember.

B. Elisha made an irrefutable commitment to God's call.
   1. We read in 1 Kings 19:21 that he left no bridge unburned.
   2. True obedience leaves no avenue for retreat.

C. In order to enjoy the obedient life we begin by a clear response to God's leading.

II. Elisha Refused to Be Discouraged (2 Kings 2:3)

A. His commitment enabled him to resist every effort to turn him aside.
   1. Elijah tried to dissuade him (vv. 2, 4 and 6).
   2. The people he met tried to dissuade him (vv. 3 and 5).

B. When we leave no road over which we could return, it is easy to resist discouragement and to stay on track with God's plan.
   1. Some people never make a complete break with their past. As a result, they struggle constantly with discouragement.
   2. Elisha never complained about the cost of his commitment.
   3. A genuine sense of direction is a valuable asset to a happy life.
   4. Elisha heard Elijah and the others but knew his assignment and stayed with it.

III. **Elisha Received the Blessing of Success (2 Kings 2:9-10, 13-15)**
   A. Elisha would not be denied. Consequently, he received a great reward.
      1. Note his request in 2 Kings 2:9-10.
      2. Note the fulfillment of that request in 2 Kings 2:11-15.
      3. His obedience had been honored.
   B. Those whose commitment is strong enough to produce an obedient life will experience special blessings from God.
      1. Note that Elisha was able to heal water that would have made the people sick (2 Kings 2:19-22).
      2. He produced water in the desert when there was none (2 Kings 3:14-20).
      3. He multiplied a widow's oil and meal (2 Kings 4:1-7).
      4. There were many other great works done through Elisha.
      5. Because of his obedience and refusal to renege on his commitment he was a great blessing to his world.

Conclusion
   A. When Elisha burned his oxen he did not know what the future held for him. He was a believer who trusted enough to act upon his belief.
   B. Those who "burn their plows" will be led of God through discouraging times to the sweet success that can only be experienced by God's obedient people.

The Danger of Living a Self-Directed Life: Saul

1 Samuel 31:1-10

Introduction

A. God had made a special arrangement with the children of Israel. They had been chosen to demonstrate to the world that there was one "Creator God."

1. In the early days, great people had been chosen to lead them in a family style relationship. Examples: Abraham, Isaac, Jacob, Moses, Joshua.
2. The next step was when they had been led by judges for 300 years. Examples: Samson, Barak, Gideon, Deborah.
3. Then came the prophets who were God's voice to provide spiritual leadership.
4. They were not content and prevailed upon God to give them a king like everyone else (1 Sam. 8).

B. While God had a better idea true to His nature to let humankind have freedom to make their choices, He consented to let them have a king.

1. That freedom to choose carried with it the responsibility for that choice.
2. God gave Israel a king like everyone else. From that king we learn a great lesson.
3. Read the scripture: 1 Sam. 31:1-10.

C. This is not a very pretty sight.

1. It is not a passage to which we turn often. But then, we do not like to look at the consequences of a self-directed life.
2. There were some beautiful days in Saul's early life as king (1 Sam. 10).

I. King Saul Had a Great Beginning

A. He had been chosen by God to be king (1 Sam. 10:1).

1. He had all of the physical qualities necessary to be a king (1 Sam. 9:2).

      2. God made sure that he knew the call was from Him
         (1 Sam. 10:6).
  B. His heart was changed (1 Sam. 10:9). This change was il-
     lustrated very distinctly in 1 Sam. 10:27.
  C. God gave Saul some special companions (v. 26).
  D. Saul had a great beginning. God tried to help him con-
     tinue in that way (12:14-15). Those words of guidance
     fell on deaf ears.

II. Saul Became a Self-Directed Man

  A. Note his confrontation with the Philistines in chapter 13.
     1. It was customary for the prophet to come and pray
       God's blessing on the army.
     2. Saul became impatient with Samuel and took matters
       into his own hands (13:11-13).
  B. This is not an unusual occurrence in the lives of self-di-
     rected people.
     1. Note Saul's pitiful excuse in 13:11-12.
     2. This still happens with people today. Impatience caus-
       es us to elevate our ideas above the guidance of God.
  C. Disobedience becomes easier the second time we face
     the option (chap. 15).

III. Look at the Results of Disobedience

  A. God withdrew His blessing and presence (15:22-26).
  B. Saul spent the rest of his days in misery.
     1. On his own, he sought help through a witch (28:4-7,
       15-20).
     2. When God leaves people to their own ways, they are
       miserable.
  C. Saul committed suicide (31:1-10).
  D. All of the potential of a great life was wasted on the altar
     of self-direction.

Conclusion

  A. It did not have to end that way. God had a better plan.
     1. Saul demonstrates what happens when self-directed
       lives come to an end.
     2. There is nowhere to turn.
  B. Where are you in relationship to God's will? Who is di-
     recting your life?

A CHOICE TO BE MADE: SAMUEL AND SAMSON

1 Samuel

Introduction

A. Today we are looking at two very famous Old Testament characters. Both of them played important roles in the history of Israel. We will examine the scripture as it relates to each one of them.

   1. Both of these men were children of promise.
   2. Their mothers had been unable to have children until God answered prayer.
   3. Both were Nazirites. That meant they could not drink alcohol or use a razor.
   4. Both of them had great beginnings.

B. In spite of their similarities the outcomes of their lives were totally different.

   1. When Samuel died after 50 years of ministry, King Joash wept.
   2. Samson was blinded by compromise, bound by the very people to whom he gave in, and he died alone.

C. The difference between these two men is very clear. It was in their choices.

I. Samuel's Choice Is Clearly Stated in 1 Sam. 3:1-10 (Read this passage.)

A. Samuel became one of the greatest men in the history of Israel.

   1. Two other famous men appear during his period— King Saul and King David.
   2. It was Samuel who anointed Saul to be the first king over Israel.
   3. It was Samuel who anointed David to succeed Saul.
   4. It is better to be a kingmaker than to be the king.

B. What was it that made Samuel such a great man?

   1. He was the product of obedient, praying parents (1 Sam. 1:21-28).

2. Notice the song of praise that Hannah sang after she took Samuel to the Temple (1 Sam. 2:1-10).
3. This reminds us of Mary's song of joy in Luke 1. Obedient people have a song.

C. Samuel grew up in the presence of the Lord (1 Sam. 2:18-21).
1. There is no substitute for being brought up in God's presence.
2. Every child should have such a heritage of faith. Unfortunately, not many do.

D. It was in that environment that Samuel developed sensitivity to God.
1. When God spoke to him, he listened (1 Sam. 3:1-10).
2. He made a deliberate choice to pursue God's will for his life.
3. Because of that choice, God was able to use him and bless him marvelously.

II. Samson, Samuel's Counterpart, Made a Different Choice (Judg. 14:1-3)

A. Look at the account of his birth in Judg. 13:2-5, 24-25.
1. Like Samuel, Samson was given a good home and a great start in life.
2. We have every reason to believe that his parents had a strong, godly home.
3. Illustration: Like any gifted athlete or musician, he was *the* "kid on the block."

B. Samson's life took a dramatic turn.
1. He came to the age when he could make dramatic, independent decisions.
2. He was in enemy territory.
3. Illustration: The environment in which we find ourselves can make it very difficult to make wise decisions.
4. He was attracted by something in enemy territory.

C. The Philistines were the enemy. Samson succumbed to temptation.
1. Living on the edge is always a formula for disaster.
2. No one envies the Samson of Judg. 16:21.
3. Disaster always follows poor choices.

Conclusion

    A. Samuel was clearly on God's side and chose to obey Him. He led a blessed life.

        1. Look at 1 Sam. 3:19; 7:10; 10:1; 15:26; 16:13.

        2. He died with honor at an old age (1 Sam. 28:3).

    B. If you had the option to live like these two men, which one would you choose?

    C. The choice is very clear. Choose to listen to God—live a great life. Choose to listen to Satan and disaster awaits.

    D. The choice is yours. Which will you choose?

A Moment of Truth: Daniel

Daniel 1:18-20

Introduction

A. Daniel was young—about 18 to 19 years of age, but he really had his life together.
  1. As result of that, the king made him a ruler over all of Babylon.
  2. He achieved a lifestyle that would be the envy of anyone.
  3. He and his friends were able to turn their world upside down (v. 17).

B. How did Daniel and his friends become so powerful and blessed?
  1. God did not just pull their names out of a hat or from a computer list.
  2. God responded to the absolute, total abandonment to their faith in Him.
  3. There is a moment of truth in the lives of all of us. This is described in Dan. 1:8-20. Read the scripture.

I. Daniel and His Friends Had a Crucial Decision to Make That Would Affect the Rest of Their Lives

A. They were in a hostile environment that they did not create.
  1. They were away from home, on their own, and responsible to no one except God.
  2. They were not looking for excuses. They had a reason for being.

B. They had self-respect, high intelligence, and the courage to stand for something.
  1. When the pressure was on (v. 5) they had their moment of truth.
  2. They could keep their faith to God's glory, or they could be like everyone else.
  3. They chose not to let the world in which they lived squeeze them into its mold (see Rom. 12:2).

4. They chose to live for something that was worthy of their very best.

II. Their Decision Was Based on Their View of What Life Is All About

A. For them, life was worthy of living for something other than being comfortable.
  1. They lived to life's fullest rather than wasting their lives as so many do.
  2. They had a deep respect for God and His guidance.
  3. If you had been in their shoes, how would you have responded?
B. Each one of us has the same choice to make.
  1. We are challenged to be like everyone else and ignore God's claim on our lives.
  2. The ultimate question is: Have we come to the place in our lives where we have enough courage, self-respect, and faith to be the very best we can be?
C. God is looking for some people He can afford to bless and use as examples.
  1. He is looking for people who do not make decisions just to be blessed.
  2. Those people will make their decisions because they are right and in line with God's will. They have the courage to be what God wants them to be.
D. This is the moment of truth that faces each one of us.
  1. This decision will give direction to the rest of our lives.
  2. Those who choose God's will never regret it.

III. Christianity Is an Epic for Heroes Only

A. It is not always comfortable, but it always has a purpose.
  1. Anyone can surrender to pressure, but it takes special people to resist.
  2. Too many choose the route of least resistance and pay dearly.
  3. Illustration: The children of Israel had a moment of truth at Canaan's border in Num. 13—14. They listened to the majority report and missed God's best.
  4. The next generation had their moment of truth. They listened to God and as a result they were blessed (Josh. 3).

B. Who do you want to emulate? The decision you make is critical to making the most out of your life.

III. Our Moment of Truth Will Give Us the Opportunity to Change Our World

A. Esther rose to her moment of truth and made a difference.
1. She was in a hostile environment through no fault of her own.
2. She took advantage of the opportunity to save her people, and she took it.
B. Because of her decision, the people were given an incredible experience (see chap. 8). When she came to her moment of truth, she chose to be different.

Conclusion

A. God has a great life planned for those who will choose to be faithful to Him.
B. Making the right choice enables us to make our world a better place to live.
C. How about you? What decision will you make?

Key to Spiritual Awakening: Jonah

Jonah 1—3

Introduction

   A. There is someone in every church who can be a key to a spiritual awakening.
- 1. This will be someone who can provide the spark to set hearts aflame for God.
- 2. If you knew that you could provide that spark, would you?

   B. The scripture we are studying today is about a city that turned to God when one man finally obeyed Him.

   C. In this passage there are several things that we should notice.
- 1. Note the need for a revival in Nineveh (1:2).
- 2. Note that there was a key person to bringing that about. His name was Jonah.
- 3. Note that the responsibility of God's call cannot be escaped (1—2).
- 4. Note that sinful people will repent when righteous people obey God's commands (3:5-9).
- 5. Note that God really wants to forgive sins (3:10).
- 6. We will read the scripture that applies to each of these points as we get to them.

I. Consider the Need for Revival (1:2)

   A. Look at Nineveh.
- 1. It was a very large city for that day. Over 120,000 people lived there.
- 2. It was the capital of Assyria. They were enemies of God's people at that time.
- 3. In its day it was the wealthiest, most splendid city in the world (Zeph. 2:15).
- 4. It was a city of great wickedness (Nah. 3:1-4).
- 5. It was a city in need of an experience with God.

   B. We are in need of a spiritual awakening today.
- 1. A look at the immorality in our country is frightening.

2. There are close parallels that could be drawn between Nineveh and today's society. We, too, are wealthy, powerful, self-sufficient, and busy.

II. The Key to the Awakening Would Be Found in Someone Who Would Mind God

A. God gave Jonah the privilege of being the key to Nineveh's revival. As described in Ezek. 22:30, God was looking for someone to stand in the gap.

B. Today God calls for people who will let Him use them to change their world.

1. The key to the awakening we need could be any one of us in this room.

2. We will never know the difference we could make unless we present ourselves wholly to God.

3. Illustration: The woman at the well was the least likely to be chosen to change her world (John 4).

III. The Responsibility of God's Call Cannot Be Avoided (1:3-17)

A. As fascinating as the story of Jonah is, because it is God's Word it is believable.

B. Jonah could not find anywhere to hide from God.

C. We cannot escape the responsibility God has for us today.

1. Like Jonah, we can run, but there is no place we can hide from God.

2. Unfortunately, as in the case of Jonah, it takes a disaster to get some to obey.

IV. Wicked People Will Repent When Righteous People Obey God (3:5-9)

A. Once the people of Nineveh heard the message, they repented. When God's representative got on track, there was something that could be done to bring a spiritual awakening to that wicked city.

B. We wonder what God could do today if we believers would obey Him.

1. The responsibility for spiritual awakening is clearly shown in 2 Chron. 7:14.

2. Many times God's hands are tied by disobedient children.

C. The world is hungry for what the Bible teaches. People are sick of religion but hungry for Jesus Christ.

V. God Wants to Forgive Sin (3:10)
A. When Nineveh heard, they repented. When they repented, God forgave.
B. This formula still works today. When unbelievers repent, God forgives.

Conclusion
A. We need to look at the world in which we live and ask ourselves if it needs a spiritual awakening.
B. Are you willing to be God's vessel to bring revival to our world?

No Place to Hide from God: Achan

Joshua 7:1-26

Introduction

A. God has been very free with His promises to humankind.
1. They cover every area of our lives.
2. Sometimes they center around outstanding events.
3. The story we are studying is such an event.
4. Read the scripture: Josh. 7:1-26.

B. As is the case with all promises, the pledge to deliver Jericho was conditional (Josh. 6:18-19).
1. God kept the promise to miraculously deliver that strong city to the Israelites.
2. Unfortunately, the Israelites broke God's conditions and took spoils.
3. When they failed to keep the conditions, God abandoned them in their next battle (Josh. 7:4-5).
4. This story teaches us an incredible lesson: We cannot hide our sins from God.

I. There Is No Hiding Place for Our Deeds

A. Look at Achan's sin (Josh. 7:21).
1. It appeared to be the perfect crime.
2. Since no one had seen Achan take the spoils, he thought no one knew.
3. The all-seeing eye of God watches everything that happens throughout the world.
4. When we fail to keep God's covenant, we are on our own (Josh. 7:4-5).
5. When judgment is passed on our sins, many people suffer.
6. In this case the Israelites and all of Achan's family paid dearly.

B. Achan's story is reenacted often in today's world.
1. The sins of one person can bring heartache to many people.

2. We cannot hide our sinful deeds from God. The price will be paid someday (Eccles. 12:14).

II. There Is No Hiding Place for the Desires of Our Hearts

A. Sin is not always what we do outwardly.
   1. Jesus made this truth very clear in the Sermon on the Mount (Matt. 5:6-7).
   2. The attitudes and desires of our hearts will have a dramatic effect upon our lives.
B. Attitudes are as important in God's sight as physical actions.
   1. God points out the importance of our attitudes in the Ten Commandments.
   2. He knows and cares about the desires of our hearts.

III. There Is No Hiding Place for Our Devotions

A. There is a major difference between desire and devotion.
   1. It was the love of wealth that caused Achan to sin.
   2. If his heart had been kept pure and focused on God, he would not have sinned.
B. Jesus taught this truth in the New Testament.
   1. In the Sermon on the Mount He warned about the danger of loving material things (Matt. 6:19-21).
   2. What we love most will determine the direction of our lives.
   3. Illustration: The story of the rich young man (Matt. 19:16-22).
C. A searching question comes to us today. What do we love most?

Conclusion

A. Achan discovered the hard way that there is no place to hide from the eyes of an all-seeing God. His failure to keep the covenant brought disaster to Achan, his neighbors, and his family.
B. God knows everything that is going on in all of our lives. When the price is paid, will others suffer for your failures? Like Achan we may confess our failures. Still, there is a high price to be paid. Since there is no hiding place for our sins, we must keep the covenant. Then we will have nothing to hide.

WHAT IS THAT IN YOUR HAND? MOSES

Exodus 4:1-17

Introduction

A. What is it that takes a tongue-tied shepherd and turns him into a powerful force strong enough to deliver God's people from slavery to the most powerful nation on earth? How is it that one man with no outstanding gifts or talents can be used of God to set His people free from the fear and abuse of their captors? Does God have similar plans to use very ordinary people today?

B. God was not pleased to see His people living in slavery and subjected to dehumanizing conditions. He was determined to deliver them. He looked for someone who would be His instrument of deliverance. He found him on the back side of the desert. God is not pleased to see His people in bondage to the ravages of sin today. He is looking for someone to deliver them. The Bible warns us in Rom. 6:23. We can defy God's Word, but we cannot defy His laws. The social chaos of our day is the result of ignoring God's moral law.

C. God is willing to change this if He can find willing people with whom to work.

I. God Chooses to Work Through Available People

A. In today's scripture God had seen His people's affliction (Exod. 3:7).
   1. Something needed to be done about their condition.
   2. God had great plans for them, but He wants help (v. 8).

B. Look at God's call upon the man He chose to help Him. Read the scripture: Exod. 4:1-17.

C. Moses—a stammering shepherd—had the opportunity to become God's instrument of change for the children of Israel.
   1. How could Moses perform this task? By using what he had.

47

     2. All that he had was an ordinary rod and an extraordinary opportunity.
     3. Moses did not have the gift of oratory (3:10).
     4. God told Him that He would make up for any deficiencies (vv. 11-12, 15).
     5. He told him to take what he had and be willing and obedient (vv. 16-17).
  D. God did everything He had promised to do.
     1. He gave Moses the words to speak in his many encounters with Pharaoh.
     2. He honored the rod as Moses obediently used it repeatedly.
     3. It was not Moses but God working through Moses' availability that brought change to their world.

II. What Is That in Your Hand?

  A. No one questions that God's highest order of creation is in trouble. We have become the slaves of sin, self, and material possessions.
  B. More and more we meet people who know absolutely nothing about God.
     1. We have the opportunity to tell them that He loves them and has a plan for them.
     2. If we reach children now, we will not have to rescue them from gangs and drugs.
     3. Teenagers need to know that they can have a close relationship with God.
     4. Adults must know that God sees them and has great plans for them.
     5. It is possible to lead our world out of the "Egyptian slavery" that is the result of sinful living into a meaningful life.

Conclusion

  A. We must use what we have to the honor and glory of God. Our rods may not be pretty or spectacular, but in the hands of obedient children of God, they can make a difference in the world. You may feel like a tongue-tied shepherd. In God's hands you can be powerful.
  B. God is looking for people who will let Him use them. How about you?

INTRODUCTION TO MESSAGES THAT CHALLENGE

The messages in this section challenge the listener to attain a higher standard of living and thereby experience a closer relationship with God. It is important to notice that it is not enough to simply be religious. These messages call for a commitment to serving God wholeheartedly.

It is very important to remember that we can never drive our listeners to be what they should be. We can only present in a meaningful way a wonderful opportunity and then challenge them to come up to the best relationship they can experience with God.

These are spiritual motivational messages.

WHY NOT THE BEST?

Malachi 1:6-14

Introduction

A. God has great plans for His people (Mal. 4:2-3). God wants His people to be free. Jesus promises freedom (John 8:36). This freedom will produce the best possible outcome for our lives.

B. Why don't all church members enjoy this wonderful experience? Many live beneath their opportunities. Many are content to just be good and religious—a formula for frustration. God has great plans for those who wish to get beyond this level of living.

C. The Book of Malachi was written during a trying time in Israel. The Jews had returned from captivity with high hopes. As years passed and nothing changed, they became disillusioned, and a spirit of depression set in. Their priests became careless about the things of God. When they began to complain, God told them to look at the real problem. Read Mal. 1:6-14.

D. The Book of Malachi was written to people who professed faith in God.
1. The challenge is still the same today (see 3:6).
2. The key verse is found in 1:14.

I. Look at the Blemished Sacrifices in Daily Living

A. It hurts to be honest, but that is the only way to know God's best (4:2).

B. God confronted them with their failure to keep their marriage covenant (2:13-16).
1. Imagine the glory that would come to God if our homes were the places of peace, joy, and love that God intended for them to be.
2. Christian homes should be Exhibit A to God's power to produce happy homes.

C. We should live in the business world with integrity. Let

those with whom we work and do business have a reason to believe in our God.

D. We should live as if God's house and service are important.

II. Look at the Blemished Sacrifices of Financial Responsibility

A. How thankful are we for the prosperity we enjoy?
1. What is the source of our energy and intelligence?
2. Do we really want to live on our own resources?
B. Remember James 1:17: "Every good and perfect gift is from above."
C. God expects the same level of faithfulness as He did from Old Testament Jews.
D. What does God expect? Look at Mal. 3:6-12. God is challenging us to test Him and see what happens.
E. We do not give in order to blessed. We give because we worship and love.

III. Look at Blemished Sacrifices Offered in Our Relationship with God and Others

A. This may be the most blatant area of weakness in Christianity.
1. We need to love God and live like it because words are cheap.
2. Note this sequence: Better Christians = better churches; better churches = better communities; better communities = a better world.
3. Is there any wonder Satan is on a crusade promoting mediocre Christianity?
4. Genuine Christianity is a supernatural walk with a living, dynamic, personal God.
B. How are you living with others? Note 1 John 4:7-8 and 20:21. Love is displayed by the characteristics of 1 Cor. 13:4-5.

Conclusion

A. God has wonderful plans for us (Mal. 4:2; John 10:10).
B. Blemished living is offering blemished sacrifices to God.
C. Why would we live beneath our privilege and fail to enjoy life at its best?

What Does God Require of Us?

Deuteronomy 10:12-13

Introduction

    A. The Christian experience is one that is alive, growing, beautiful, and exciting.

        1. It can be compared to a beautiful love affair that dramatically affects a life.

        2. Some people who fall in love with God do not know what God expects of them.

        3. The fact is that none of us knew all of the details when we accepted Him as Lord.

        4. With this in mind, we will look at this passage of scripture today.

        5. Read the scripture: Deut. 10:12-13.

    B. Look at the background of this scripture.

        1. To fully understand it, we need to know why this passage of scripture was given.

        2. Consider Moses' experience.

            a. The people had received mercy from God for their sin in making the golden calf.

            b. After breaking the first set of tablets, Moses had another meeting with God.

            c. He had received a new set and had a new opportunity for them.

        3. In view of all that had happened Moses was letting them know what God expected of them.

    C. There are four simple requirements in this scripture that are appropriate for every believer to remember.

I. Fear the Lord Your God (v. 12)

    A. We cannot help but adore His majesty, stand in awe of His power, and dread His wrath. But in this passage we see that something else is expected of us.

        1. Fear as it is used here does not mean the same as to run and hide. It means to have a holy reverence and deep respect for God.

    2. Devout Israelites had a deep respect for God. He had chosen and kept them.
  B. Those of us who love God will have a "wholesome" respect for Him.
    1. It is critical that we have a holy reverence and show that by the way we live.
    2. This is just the beginning of a healthy relationship. We soon move on to the second challenge.

II. Walk in His Ways (v. 12)

  A. Through Moses, God gave the children of Israel simple commandments.
    1. Human nature demands clear guidelines.
    2. Illustrate: We must have traffic and speed laws to keep us safe on our highways.
    3. If God had not given the Ten Commandments to us, we would have no distinct direction for our lives.
    4. Knowing humanity as He does, God has given us what we need to not only please Him but also to enjoy a good world.
  B. In 1 John 5:3, we are sensitized to the fact that God's commands are not a burden.
    1. John wrote that loving God and keeping His commandments are inseparable.
    2. What is so difficult about loving God, honoring His name, and worshiping Him?
    3. What is so difficult about being honest, peaceful, considerate of others, and so forth?
  C. Walking in His ways is not a problem. It is a beautiful way in which to live.

III. Love Him (v. 12)

  A. We must fear Him as a great and sovereign God, but love Him as a good God and our benefactor.
    1. God knew that to physically observe the commandments could be a dull, legalistic, meaningless experience.
    2. Therefore, He added the reason we do all that we do—love.
  B. If we take love out of any dimension of our lives, life becomes oppressive.

IV. Serve Him (v. 12)

A. There is a difference between keeping the commandments and serving Him.

   1. Keeping the commandments can be a legalistic, factual approach to God.

   2. Service, the language of love, goes beyond the letter of the law.

B. There are innumerable ways to serve God. Find something you do not have to do and do it for the glory of God.

Conclusion

A. In John 21:15-19 Jesus challenged Peter to exhibit His love.

B. God is simply asking us to love Him, trust Him, walk with Him, and serve Him.

C. Will you follow these simple requirements that God has for your life?

THE WAY OUT IS UP

2 Chronicles 7:12-22

Introduction

A. The promise in today's scripture comes when Solomon was dedicating the Temple. They were going through a period of progress (see chap. 8). They were enjoying a time of peace (see chap. 9). It was a period of unparalleled prosperity (see 9:13-28).

B. The Temple was the evidence that things were going well with Israel. Yet, at the time of dedication, God had a special message. Read 2 Chron. 7:12-22.

C. God has always been fair with humankind. He attempted to alert them to temptations they would face (v. 19). He told them the price of yielding to those temptations (v. 20). He told them in advance what the solution to that problem would be (v. 14).

D. However, the next generation began to turn away from God and paid a high price. King Rehoboam did evil because he did not seek the Lord (2 Chron. 12:14). The country was split between Judah and Israel, and problems plagued them. In 2 Chron. 20, one story concerning Judah has a great message for us.

I. Look at the Admission of Need

A. Judah was faced with an enemy that they could not handle (vv. 1-2).

    1. There could be no progress toward a solution until the need was acknowledged.

    2. Jehoshaphat was wise and sought help from God.

B. Our world is battling an enemy that is much too great for us. The moral decay, mayhem in the streets, and hatred in our world are more than we can handle alone. Those who want a life of peace, progress, and prosperity face an enemy of overwhelming odds.

II. Is There a Solution to the Problems People Face?
A. Judah remembered the promise of 2 Chron. 7:14.
1. Look at the example given in 2 Chron. 20:6-14.
2. God responded with an answer (vv. 15-17).
3. He is simply telling them that if they would trust Him enough to show it through the way they lived, He would take care of them.
B. God is saying the same thing to us today.
1. He is telling us to trust Him, live like it, and He will make up the difference.
2. It is significant that the message came to the people who were called by His name.
3. When believers live according to what they believe, the world will pay attention.

III. Look at the Results of Absolute Faith in God
A. The children of Israel marched into battle with a confident spirit.
1. They did not go with fear and trembling but with faith and a song (v. 21).
2. In verse 21 we read that when their faith was evidenced, God fought for them.
3. Remember His promise in 2 Chron. 7:14. When the children of Israel carried out verses 15 and 17, God responded.
B. This is still our only hope.
1. There is no earthly power that can deliver us.
2. Without God's help we will not be able to win this battle ourselves.
3. We face an overwhelming enemy who has a vast army marching against us.
4. Our hope for victory is through a fresh outpouring of God's presence.

Conclusion
A. Notice when God began to move (2 Chron. 20:22). They had prayed (v. 6). God had given them instructions (v. 15). They believed (v. 20). He delivered them (vv. 22-23). The result of following His guidance is joy in the camp (vv. 26-29).
B. This same thing can happen in our world today. The way out of the problem is found in looking up at Him.

A Choice to Be Made

Joshua 1:10-18; 3:14-17

Introduction

    A. The life we live is the result of the choices we make.

        1. Every choice has a price. There is no free lunch.

        2. Illustration: I have a choice to stop at a red light and waste time or to run the light and to pay for that choice with an accident or a ticket.

        3. We can choose to be moral and live holy lives or live immorally and pay a price.

        4. Because of the importance of the choices we make we will look at two experiences of the children of Israel and the consequences of those choices.

        5. Read the scripture: Josh. 1:10-18; 3:14-17.

    B. The contrast in these scriptures is worthy of serious study. It has been said that happiness is a choice. It is also true that we have control over our personal attitudes.

    C. Look at the results of making a positive choice to obey God. In Isa. 1:19, we are promised to receive blessings when we are obedient. This is clearly indicated in today's scripture.

I. There Are Some Things That Encourage Us to Be Obedient

    A. Remember what God has done in the past.

        1. The Israelites needed to remember His power in parting the Red Sea (Exod. 13:17-22 and 14:19-28).

        2. Remember God's provision during the wilderness days (Deut. 29:5-15). It was greatly encouraging to read what God had done in the wilderness.

    B. It will help us to look at what God has done for us.

        1. The Red Sea was the Israelites' deliverance from bondage.

        2. The wilderness was a purifying process where they learned lessons in obedience.

3. The Promised Land was a maturing experience that God wants for all of us.
C. Reflecting on God's grace helps our attitudes.
   1. Remember that grace is unmerited favor.
   2. We can learn lessons in obedience from the Israelites' wilderness experiences. Follow the cloud God placed above. Gather the manna one day at a time to keep it from spoiling.
D. We need to relight the fire within our souls.
   1. Choosing to obey produced wonderful experiences for the Israelites.
   2. Illustration: The defeat of Jericho came about through their obedience.
   3. The attitude of Joshua was contagious.
E. We can choose to obey and trust God's love, power, and wisdom, or we can go in our own power and die in the wilderness.

II. Many Problems Are Created by Disobedience
A. We can see some of the problems in Num. 13 and 14.
   1. The Israelites are at the edge of Canaan. They are at the end of the desert.
   2. God's best is very close for them (Num. 13:26-27).
B. The problem is that they had developed some bad attitudes. Illustration: Miriam and Aaron in Num. 12. They had forgotten how strong they are with God's help (Num. 13:31-39). They had forgotten what God had done for them (Deut. 29:5-6).
C. Forgetting God's goodness is the first step toward bad attitudes and choices. God resents bad attitudes. (Num. 14:11 and 18:24).

Conclusion
A. Listen to God's Word in Num. 14:36-38. What kind of attitude are you spreading? The choice is yours. Be assured, your choice has a price tag.
B. We stand at the edge of our "Jordan." We can pay the price of faith and obedience and make the right choice. Or we can display a bad attitude, make poor choices, and pay dearly. What choice will you make?

CONFRONTING CASUAL CHRISTIANITY

Ezekiel 22:23-31

Introduction
A. The most pressing need of the Church is for those who carry the Lord's name to live a life of total commitment to Him.
   1. Many people are willing to give up their sins and be religious.
   2. The Church struggles with four Cs that are present in many believers' lives: complacency, criticism, coolness to the things of God, coldness toward other believers.
   3. If Jesus had felt toward His opportunity to provide redemption for us as so many feel toward others, we would still be without salvation.
B. Today's society is committed to the cult of comfort.
   1. The call of God is totally opposite (Matt. 16:24-25).
   2. We must not forget that those who follow the path of total commitment follow the bloodstained footsteps of Jesus into the presence of the Father.
C. In today's scripture God is trying to arouse His people to serious service.
   1. Read the scripture: Ezek. 22:23-31.
   2. Along with King Jehoiakim, Ezekiel had been taken captive by the Babylonians.
   3. The Israelites had relied on their alliance with Egypt to protect and preserve them.
   4. Ezekiel shows the folly of looking anywhere except to God for delivery from evil.
   5. In verse 30, God is looking for people who care enough to be involved.
D. In this message we are going to look at two simple questions:
   1. What is the problem?
   2. What is the solution?
   3. If we do not see the problem, we will not understand the need for a cure.

I. The Problem Is in Having a Casual Approach to Christianity

A. Two serious statements:
1. Indifference within the ranks of many church people is more destructive to God's work than any organized outside force.
2. Western Christianity is too weak and ineffective to make a significant difference in the battle for the world.
3. These are serious charges and explain why many do not accept our message.

B. It is understood that the Church has survived to this point because of those who are committed, faithful, and accountable. Two illustrations:
1. In too many cases, the Church is like a team where some play their hearts out while others sit on the bench.
2. The Church can be like a motor where some cylinders work and others do not. Those who live casual Christian lives extract a lot of strength from those who are totally involved in the work of the Kingdom.

C. This may sound like strong medicine, but that may be what it takes to be well.
1. Illustration: The more serious our illness may be, the stronger our medicine.
2. As your spiritual physician who wants you to be healthy, take the whole dosage.

II. Look at the Cure for the Problem

A. The cure begins with an honest look at ourselves.
1. Am I what I profess to be and should be?
2. Am I what Jesus died for me to be?
3. If I were to die, would there be a missing link between God and my world?

B. There is no such thing as a partial commitment.
1. Illustration: Upon taking off, an airplane reaches a point of no return.
2. Unfortunately, there are many church members who have been sitting on the runway gunning their engines for years but never leaving the ground.

C. Who Is in charge of your life?
   1. Since you were saved, has there been a time when you totally committed to Him?
   2. You were not forgiven to sit at the end of the runway and think about flying. You were made to fly!
   3. Paul gives clear guidance to what needs to happen in our lives (Rom. 12:1).
   4. Christians do not have the right to live their own lives and do their own thing. If the God of the Bible is our God, He has final authority over our lives.

Conclusion
A. God wants to bless you, but He will not unless you love Him enough to demonstrate that He is the top priority in your life.
B. God is looking for people to fulfill Ezek. 22:30.
C. How about you? Will you stand in the gap?

The High Cost of Compromise

Judges 2—3

Introduction

  A. The children of Israel were very special to God.
    1. He freed them from Egyptian slavery because He had better plans for them.
    2. He guided them across a trackless desert to the edge of Canaan.
    3. He was patient with them. After 40 years they crossed into the Promised Land.
    4. As they entered Canaan, each of the 12 tribes was given a special place as well as an assignment to fulfill in order to continue to receive God's blessings.
    5. In Exod. 23:23-33 God made a special covenant with them.
  B. Today's Christian church represents the Israelites, and the various denominations represent the different tribes.
    1. While we may have differences, we have one assignment.
    2. That is to glorify God.
  C. The children of Israel struggled constantly with faithfulness and compromise.
    1. They paid a high price for failure and enjoyed great blessings for faithfulness.
    2. We must learn from their experiences, which will help us stay true to God.
    3. We will read the scripture as it applies to each of the lessons.

I. Lesson One: There Is a Divine Assignment (2:1-3)

  A. Notice the strength of God's covenant.
    1. God demanded that they remain separate from the people with whom they mixed.
    2. Remember God's command in Exod. 34:12-17.
    3. In verse 2 we read that they broke the contract with God.

        4. Nonbelievers were a constant source of trouble to the Israelites.

        5. There can be no peaceful coexistence between godliness and ungodliness.

   B. Unbelievers are a constant source of irritation to those who draw clear lines of commitment to God.

        1. Once we settle this question, we will not vacillate between right and wrong.

        2. It is easy to keep the divine assignment when we draw firm lines of commitment.

II. Lesson Two: We Can Learn from a Desperate Problem (2:7-9)

   A. Joshua, the leader who had led them into the Promised Land, had died.

        1. The man of commitment, courage, and faith was gone.

        2. That generation had kept the faith, but they also died (v. 10).

        3. The next generation wanted to enjoy privileges of the land without keeping the covenant (vv. 10-13).

        4. In verse 17 we read about what happens when God's covenant is broken.

   B. The further we get away from our spiritual covenant, the more desperate our problems become.

        1. When we forget what God has done in the past we end up worshiping the "idols" of our neighbors.

        2. We are under special assignment to be different from the rest of the world.

III. Lesson Three: Distance Brings Disaster (3:5-7)

   A. As they lived among the heathens and became familiar with them, the Israelites lost their identity.

        1. When they intermarried with the forbidden people, they encountered trouble.

        2. They began to worship heathen idols (3:6-7).

   B. The lesson is simple. The further we move from our foundation and closer to the world around us, we, too, can lose our identity as God's children.

        1. They were Israelites but no longer represented God to the world.

        2. So it can become with us.

IV. Lesson Four: There Is an Answer (3:9)

A. When the Israelites turned to God, He responded.
1. When they lived like His people, He blessed them.
2. When they turned away from Him, the cost was enormous (4:1-3).

B. Will we ever learn these lessons?

Conclusion

A. We have nothing to lose by being God's special people. But we cannot move in and out of the covenant relationship.

B. The cost of compromising our position is higher than any of us can afford to pay.